VIENNA

VIENNA • VIENNE • VIENA

Second revised and expanded edition

Postcard-publisher • Touristinformation-publisher
A-1180 Vienna • Kutschkergasse 42 • Tel: 0222/47686
Telefax: 47686-21
Telex: 13 27 41 Kuhna

Published by Gerd-Volker Weege in collaboration with Eveline Kozma and Christine Pomberger • Translations: Mike Langley (english) • Mag. Maria Elena Schimanovich (italian) • Anrea Mayr and Claudia Schimansky (spanish) • Jocelyne Gan (french) Photographs: Wolfsberger, Matthias Fiegl, Volker Weege, Albertina's Graphic Collection, Kunsthistorisches Museum, Österreichischer Bundestheaterverband Opernballbüro, Society for the Preseruation of the Kapuziner Crypt, Österreichische Galerie, Josef Palffy, Fleischmann & Mair • Typesetting: partners®, Vienna • Printing and Production: Alpina, Innsbruck

CONTENTS

from top to buttom:
Cathedral of St. Stephan
National Opera
Imperial Theater
Museum of Art History

4

from top to buttom:
Hofburg
Palace Schönbrunn
Giant Ferris Wheel in the Prater
Hundertwasser-House
Heuriger

with its unique Lipizzans, the New Year's Concert, the Festwochen (Festival Weeks), the Opera Ball (which is televised in many countries), or the famous Sachertorte (Sacher cake) made originally by the legendary, cigar-smoking Anna Sacher. A typical Viennese is hard to describe. Often he complains about God and the world, griping constantly. On the other hand he embodies the very idea of loveableness. Generally, „der liebe Augustin" is a symbol for the Viennese. According to the story, Augustin was a jolly soul who stayed happy despite the Black Plague's destruction all around him, armed with a glass of wine, facing his fate and death. A more critical Viennese character, „Herr Karl", was created by Qualtinger and Merz for the stage. „Herr Karl" embodies the pushy artist of life with pessimistic brutality.

The story of the federal capital Vienna is a reflection of Austria's past. Beginning with the trade route between north and south, the Bernsteinstraße over the Semmering (which was used by the Celts), the Roman Castrum Vindobona was expanded in the first century as a border fortress against the Germanic tribes. In 213 A. D. Vindobona became a Roman city. After the Avar Wars (791–796) the Ostmark was founded by Charlemagne. The name „Ostarriche" appeared for the first time on a document in 996. The appellation „Wenia" can be traced back to 881. Under Duke Heinrich II, Austria became a duchy, according to the „Privilegium minus" around 1156. The offices of government moved from Regensburg to Vienna. Accordingly, the expansion of the city and the construction of a new wall, the „Ringmauer", was necessary. In 1221 Vienna received medieval city rights. After the defeat of the Bohemian King and sovereign Ottokar II in the battle of Marchfeld (1276), the history of Vienna and Austria was inseparably connected to the House of Habsburg. Vienna received its university in 1365. A golden age for the city began in 1439. The seat of the Holy Roman Empire in Vienna (until 1806) had cultural and economical effects on the city. Habsburg rule was interrupted from 1485–90 by the Hungarian Matthias Cor-

HISTORY OF VIENNA

Vienna, the former Imperial city and melting pot of many nations, is one of the diversest of Europe's cities. Many cultural, political and ethnic influences have left their mark on this metropolis and made it incomparable to other cities. Seen politically, Vienna lies before the gateway to the East, with which it has had good relations, even before recent liberalization tendencies. Geographically it lies in the heart of Europe, or is the heart of Europe, as Vienna generally considers itself. In the „city of the waltz" there are many attractions known worldwide and visited by tourists from near and far – be it Schönbrunn, Belvedere, numerous museums and theatres (such as the Burgtheater, one of the oldest and richest in tradition in the world), the Vienna Philharmonic Orchestra, the Sängerknaben, the Spanische Hofreitschule

vinus. After the Peace of Preßburg, an Austrian, Emperor Maximilian I, came to power (1493–1519), acquiring what is now Schloß Schönbrunn. The Farmers' Uprisings (1525), the wars of religion and the Counterreformation were followed by two Turkish invasions (1529 and 1683), both of which were successfully held back. Numerous catholic clergymen (Servites, barefoot Karmelites, Augustinites and Barnabites) were called to Vienna in the 17th century, and they built many churches in the center of town. Nothing more stood in Vienna's way to becoming a metropolis. The baroque style and the clever ruler, Maria Theresia (1740–1780), as well as her son, Joseph II (1780–1790) brought a real Golden Age to the city. Alongside great musicians and poets, excellent architects such as Johann Lukas von Hildebrand and Johann Berhard and his son, Josef Emanuel Fischer von Erlach were at work, forming the city's image with magnificent buildings. Haydn, Mozart, Gluck and, later, Beethoven and Schubert founded Vienna's reputation as the music capital of Europe. Napoleon's entry brought a short decline (1805 and 1809), but the Congress of Vienna (1814–15) brought a new Golden Age, bringing together Europe's leaders in Vienna. A new map of the continent was drawn in a time of wild parties („The Congress dances!") as the Wiener Walzer (Vienna Walzer) was established as an art-form and Metternich steered the history of Austria.

The opposition between the well-to-do citizens and the lower classes came to a head in the Biedermeier era, with a revolution in 1848. Emperor Franz Ferdinand I had to abdicate in favor of the 18-year-old Franz Joseph I, who ruled the country 68 years (1848–1916). During his rule, the Austro-Hungarian monarchy's population grew to 50 million. He ordered the Ringstraße to be built in the 1870's as well as the second Viennese water pipeline in 1910. He and his Bavarian wife Elisabeth, known as „Sissy", are among the most legendary of Austria's ruling couples. Their reign had many highlights, such as the „Era of Golden Operettas" with Strauß, Suppe, Zeller, Ziehrer, and Millöcker. At the same time, however, nationalism and separatism began to shake the foundations of the multi-ethnic state, leading to the first World War (1914–1918). Franz Joseph I did not witness the fall of the monarchy, having died in 1916. His successor, Karl I, refused the throne in 1918, and the First Republic came to power.

After the confusion of World War One, Vienna became the federal capital in 1918 and a federal „state" (Bundesland) in 1922. Adolf Hitler marched into Austria in 1938 after the worldwide economic crisis. World War Two followed with devasting results for Vienna. The capital was bombed many times, and many valuable buildings were destroyed, some of which were be repaired or replaced after 1945. The National Contract was signed in Schloß Belverdere in 1955, and the occupational forces of Russia, Great Britain, USA and France left Austria. From this point on, Austria was a free, neutral state.

Today, more than 40 years after the Second World War, Vienna has changed somewhat. The capital of a small, neutral country has arisen from the metropolis of a large state. Vienna remains, the center of European music, with its world-renowned Wiener Festwochen (Festival Weeks) and the annual New Year's concert by the Vienna Philharmonic Orchestra. Vienna's reputation and value as a center for international relations have remained, also. Since 1979, Vienna has hosted the third seat of the UNO, behind New York and Geneva. Today, around 1,5 million people live in Vienna in an area of 414,56 square kilometers.

Because of its favorable location, Vienna is the site of conventions, and the atmosphere of the city contributes to its guests' feeling of well-being, either at one of many cultural events, political or economic conventions, or simply on vacation.

MONUMENTS IN THE INNER CITY

Gestaltung: Heinz Schwanninger

Sehenswürdigkeiten
Places of interest
Curiosités
Edifici più importanti
1:10000

0   100   200m

Leopoldsg.

Obere Donaustraße

Sigmund-Freud-Museum
Berggasse
Türken — straße
Straße
Franz-
Josefs-
ring
Ringturm
Börse

Schotten-
gasse
Wipplinger
straße
Kolin-
Maria-Theresien-

DONAUKANAL

Heinrichsgasse
Salzgries
Maria am Gestade
Wipplingerstr.
Altes Rathaus
Marc-Aurel-Straße
Lessing-Dkm.
St. Ruprecht

Obere Donaustraße
Untere Donaustraße
Holland-
straße
straße

Tabor-
straße
Prater-
straße

Hl. Josef
straße

Johannes der Täufer
Kirche d. Barmherzigen
Brüder

Aspernbrücke
Urania
Franz-Josefs-Kai

universität
Beethoven-
Pasqualatihaus
Lieben-
bergdenkmal

Neidhart-
Fresken-Haus
Schottenkirche
Schottenhof
Melker-
hof
Palais
Kinsky
Palais
Batthyány
Clemens-
Hofbauer-
Dkm.

Schotten-
gasse
Freyung
Tiefer
Graben
Am Hof
Bürgerliches
Zeughaus
Palais Collalto
Marien-
säule
Salvatorkap.

Ankeruhr
Vermählungs-
brunnen
Hoher
Markt
Römische
Ruinen

Griechen-
gasse
straße

Dreifaltig-
keitskirche
Heiligenkreuzer
Hof
Gutenberg-
Dkm.
St.
Barbara

Dominikanerbastei
ring

Radetzky
Dkm.
Regierungs-
gebäude
Marxer
Gasse
Stuben-
ring
Zollamts-
straße
Hintere Zollamtsstr.

Burgtheater
Minoriten-
kirche
Niederöster.
Landesmus.
Palais
Harrach
Palais
Liechten-
stein
Palais II -
Palais
Kinsky

Herren
gasse
Naglergasse
Kohl-
markt
Graben
Tuch-
lauben

Kirche
Am Hof
Uhrenmuseum
Peterskirche
Pestsäule

Josefs-
brunnen

Dom-
museum
St.
Alte
Schmiede

Universitäts-
kirche
Jesuitenkirche
Stephansdom
Virgilkapelle
Wollzeile
Rotenturm-
straße

Dominikaner-
kirche

Weiskirchner-
str.
Landstraßer Hauptstr.
Invaliden-
straße
gasse

Volks-
museumstempel
garten
Alte
Hofburg
Heldenplatz
Fiaker
Burgtor
Maria-
theresien-
Pl.
ring

Bundes-
kanzleramt
Loos-
haus
Michaeler-
pl.
Michaelerkirche

Schaufler-
g.
Span. Hof-
reitschule
Josefs-
Dorotheum
Kaiser
Josef II -
Dkm.
Konvikt
Augustiner
kirche
Albertina

Leopolds-
brunnen
Neuer
Markt
Donner-
brunnen
Kapuziner-
gruft
Stock im
Eisen
Deutsche
Ordens
Palais
Neupauer-
Bräuner
Franziskaner-
kirche

Palais-
Fürstenberg
Stubenbastei
Dr.-Karl-
Lueger-Dkm.

Fiaker
Mozart-
Erinnerungsräume
Stuben-
straße

Österreichisches
Museum für
angewandte
Kunst

Handelswasserhaus
Krehlgasse. 44

Erzherzog
Karl-Dkm.
Schatz-
kammer
Nationalbibliothek
Neue
Hofburg
Burggarten
Fiaker

Kärntner Str.
Singer-
straße

Palais-Erdödy-
Fürstenberg
Malteser
Kirche
Johannes-
gasse
stätte

Zelinka-Dkm.
Schubert-

Makart-

Johann-
Strauß-
Dkm.
Stadtpark
Kursalon
Seb.-Kneipp-
Haupt-
münzamt

Burgtheater
gartenmuseum

Burg-
garten
Theatermus.
Goethe-
Dkm.
Staatsoper

Franz-
Josef-Dkm.

St. Ursula
Hofkammer-
archiv
St. Anna
Kremsmünster-
hof

Seiler-
stätte
Schwarzenbergstr.

Am Heumarkt
Beatrix
gasse
gasse

Opern-
ring
Kunsthistorisches
Museum

Schiller-
Dkm.
Kärntner Ring
Beethoven-
Dkm.

Salesianer-
gasse

Getreidemarkt
Straße
Kunst-
akademie
Friedrichstr.
Sezession
Opern-
gasse
Künstler-
haus
Musik-
verein
Lothringer
Akad
Theater
Am Heumarkt
Konzerthaus
Straße

Schwarzen-
berg-Dkm.
Zaunerg.

Neuling

Theater
a. d. Wien
Nibelungen-
gasse
Girardi-Dkm.
Otto-Wagner-
Karlsplatz

Madersperger
Dkm.
Brahms-
Dkm.
Donner-
Dkm.
Histor. Museum
der Stadt Wien
Schwarzenbergpl.
Serb.-
kirche
Russ.
Kirche

Naschmarkt
Linke Wienzeile
Rechte Wienzeile
Wiedner Haupt-
Opern-
gasse

Technische
Universität
Karlskirche

Hochstrahl-
Russisches
Helden-Dkm.
Hofmannsthal-
Geburtshaus

Gardekirche
Palais
Schwarzenberg
Unt. Belvedere

MONUMENTS
OUTSIDE THE CITY

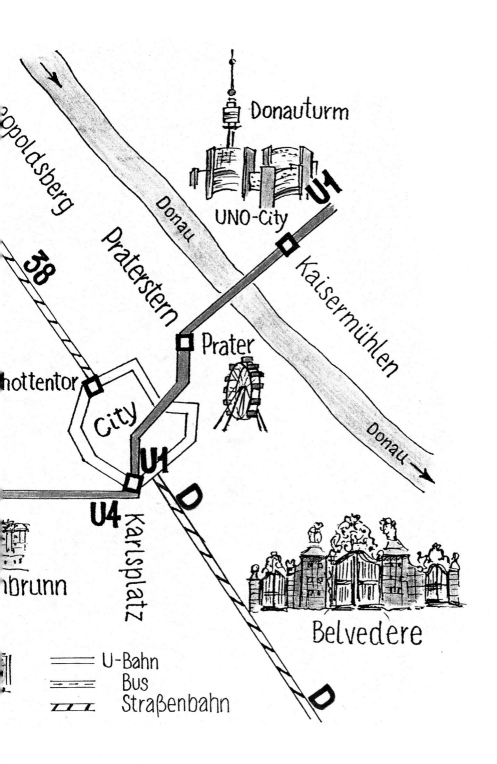

Donauturm

UNO-City

U1

Leopoldsberg

Donau

Praterstern

Kaisermühlen

38

Prater

Schottentor

City

Donau

U1

D

U4

Karlsplatz

brunn

Belvedere

D

U-Bahn
Bus
Straßenbahn

Schnellverbinc

U1 U-Bahn-Linie

S 1 Schnellbahnlinie

Lokalbahn Wien-Baden

B3 Busbahnhof

Kundenzentrum
der Wiener Linien
(U3-Station Erdberg)

i Informationsstelle
der Wiener Linien

V Vorverkaufsstelle

gen in Wien

Strebersdorf
Jedlersdorf
Brünner Straße
V i S15 B3
Siemens-straße
S2 Gerasdorf
U6 Floridsdorf
Leopoldau
Süßenbrunn
S1
Strandbäder
ridsdorfer
icke
Neue Donau
S45
Handelskai
Traisengasse
U1 B3 V
Kagran
Hausfeldstraße S80
Hirschstetten
Aspern
Alte Donau
Kaisermühlen-
Vienna Int. Centre
Donauinsel
Erzherzog-Karl-Straße
Roßauer
Lände
Vorgartenstraße
Nestroypl.
Praterstern (Wien Nord)
S7 V i
Stadlau
U2
V
Schottenring
Schwedenpl.
V
Stephanspl.
Stubentor
B3
S7 V i
Landstraße
(Wien Mitte)
Lobau
V
i
Rochusgasse
V
Kardinal-Nagl-Platz
Stadtpark
i
Schlachthausgasse
Stadlauer Brücke
Lusthaus
Karlsplatz
U3 Erdberg
V B3
Taubstummen-gasse
Rennweg
Südtiroler
Platz
S80
S60
V
Simmering
Aspang-bahn
Haidestraße
Südbahnhof
Simmeringer Hauptstraße
Keplerplatz
Zentralfriedhof
Zentralfriedhof Klederling
Reumannplatz
U1 B3 V
Simmering
Ostbahn
Klein Schwechat
Groß Schwechat
rf-Siebenhirten
Klederling
S60
S7

13

above left:
Master Pilgram

above right:
Coat of Arms on the Roof

below left:
Pulpit

below right:
Emperor Friedrich III's Crypt

right side:
Cathedral of St. Stephan

CATHEDRAL OF ST. STEPHAN

One of the most monumental of Vienna's architectural structures is obviously the *Stephansdom*, which towers over the inner city. On this site stood the romanesque basilica founded in the 12th century by Duke Heinrich

II. Jasomirgott. After fire-damage in 1258, the church was rebuilt in romanesque style. The round-arched Giant Gate and the later lightly gothi- cized Heathen's Towers are still to be seen today. The cornerstone for the gothic

14

Stephanskirche was laid in April 1359 under Rudolf IV., also called „the Donor". The south tower was made by Hans v. Prachatitz (1433), and the nave by Hanns Puchsbaum (1455). The gothic roof framework was destroyed in the last days of World War Two, but it was renewed after much difficulty. „Der Steffl", as the 137 meter high tower (Stephansturm) is lovingly called by the Viennese, is their city's landmark and one of the greatest achievements

Wiener Neustädter Altar

of gothic architecture. The Tower Room (72 meters high) was once used by the fire department. Albrecht I, the German king, began the construction of the gothic cathedral in 1304 and added the „Albertinischen" Choir (named after himself) onto the romanesque basilica. Remains of the original window (made of glass) are now mounted in the central apse window. The middle choir is dedicated to Christ and St. Stephan, the north choir to Mary, and the south

Inner View of St. Stephan's Cathedral

choir to the apostles. Rudolf the Donor succeeded in emancipating the Vienna parish from the Bishop of Passau through the establishment of a collegiate donation and a brotherhood of priests led by a clergyman from the imperial sovereign. This important step was documented in the contruction of the gothic nave.

The „Pummerin" is one of the world's largest bells. It was made in 1711 from the metal of captured Turkish cannons and hung originally

Organ

High Altar

in the south tower. During the fire of 1945 it fell and shattered, but out of the shards a new bell was made in St. Florian in Upper Austria. Ever since 1952, the „Pummerin" greets the New Year at midnight on December 31 from the north tower.

Its diameter is 314 cm and it heighs 21,4 tons. The inside of the cathedral spans a 27 meter high webbed-arch which is carried by 18 pillars. The High Altar was constructed by Johann Jakob Pock (1640–1647) and is worked in black marble, with thin plates car-

rying depictions of the stoning of St. Stephanus, the first Christian martyr. Much more important is the Wiener Neustädter Altar, located in the left nave. The gothic winged altar dates back to 1447.

In the central reliquary are depictions of the crowning of Mary, St. Barbara and St. Katharina. The life of Mary and Jesus adorns the inner side. AEIOU are the initials of Friedrich III's election slogan, „Alles Erdreich ist Österreich Untertan" (The Earth is subservient to Austria). His sarcophagus, designed by Niclas Ger-

18

Dienstbotenmadonna

Seitenaltar

haert van Leyden, is cut in red marble and stands in the right nave. The „Riesenorgel" (Giant Organ) has four keyboards, 125 registers and about 10.000 pipes, and is one of Europe's biggest organs. Its creator, Anton Pilgrim, immortalized himself in a bust at the late-gothic foot of the organ.

Another Pilgrim self-portrait is located at the base of the pulpit he made of sandstone in 1514/15. This portrait is known as the „Fenstergucker" (window-gawker). On the gothic pulpit's stairs, carved toads and lizards, symbols of evil, are hindered by a dog, symbol of good. The Capistran pulpit, erected in 1430, is another example of gothic architecture. The Franciscan Johannes Capestrano called out here in 1451 for the crusade against the Turks. In the catacombs, also called crypts, the entrails of many Habsburgers are buried. Their hearts are in the Loretto chapel in St. Augustin, and their bodies lie in the Kapuziner crypt.

KARLSKIRCHE

The most important baroque church construction in Vienna was begun in 1716 by Johann Bernhard Fischer von Erlach and finished in 1739 by his son Joseph Emanuel. In 1713, as the Plague was raging for the seventh time in Vienna, killing around 8000 people, Emperor Karl IV made a vow to the Saint of the Plague, Karl Borromäus, that he would build a church as soon as Vienna were freed of the horrible scourge. In 1714 the Plague was over, and work began without delay on an imposing, imperial house of God.

Cardinal Sigismund Graf Kollonitz, Archbishop of Vienna, performed consecration ceremonies in October 1737, and Vienna now had received a work of architecture that would forever be a monumental landmark. The mighty front of the church is a rich and complex structure, which the architect had developed from his conceptions of „Historical Architecture" (1721).

The church was based on Fischer von Erlach's exact knowledge of classical Greek and Roman architecture as well as on his studies of French and Italian design. As such the following features are recognizable: the central 72m high circular part with cupola, the protruding pillars in the form of Greek temples, both 47m high depictive pillars (similar to the Roman Trajan's Pillar), and the gate-pavilions on either side. The round drum of the central area stretches from the shining copper cupola, distinguished by a crowning tambour. The pillared hall is commanded by Karl Borromäus who thrusts his face forward. On the other sides, like a flank of cyclopic guards, the spiral pillars twist around. The motion turns back and is sucked into the depths. The rear section of this hallway-like structure are high-baroque, the protruding sections are in classical-antique form. The total concept is that of a widely-piled pyramid. Visitors can clearly see that the architect planned here a wonderful building in universal, holy and imperial taste in the resi-

right:
Inner View of the Karlskirche

dence of a world empire. The entryway into the church is flanked by two powerful angels with bronze crucifixes. The relief in the flat triangular gable of the front area depicts shocking scenes of Vienna's misery at the time of the Plague. Karl Borromäus, who alleviated the suffering through powerful prayers, crowns the gable. The most important artists of the period contributed to the inner decoration. Sculptors such as Lorenzoi Mattieli, Giovanni Stanetti, Johann Baptist Straub, Jakob Schletter and many others created the figurative ornamentation in the church. Daniel Gran painted the altar-picture of the baptismal chapel to the left of the main entrance, Martin Altomonte painted that of the chapel across on the right. Johann Michael Rottmayr's monumental cupola frescoes with

a depiction of the „Glory of St. Borromäus" are a witness to the Counterreformation's victory. The High Altar is by the master Fischer von Erlach himself. In 1738 Karl VI gave the Karlskirche to the Order of the Kreuzherren, which looks after it still today.

MARIA AM GESTADE

Maria am Gestade („Maria on the shore"), also called the „Czechish National Church", was built between 1330 and 1414. The original romanesque church of the 13th century burned down.

During the Napoleonic wars, it served as a military camp. The foundation of the devotionals are the remains of old Roman city walls. The 56m high tower is built on a seven-cornered base, and belongs, along with its rich filigree-decorated crest, to the most beautiful remaining examples of gothic Vienna. The colorful glass windows date back to the 15th century.

VOTIVKIRCHE

As thanks for the failure of an assassination attempt on the emperor, Archduke Ferdinand Maximilian had the Votivkirche built, and it was dedicated on the Silver Wedding Anniversary of the Imperial couple, Franz Joseph I. and Elisabeth in 1879. The construction was made according to plans by Johann Heinrich von Ferstel in the historicizing New Gothic style (with three naves and two 99m high towers).

The „Antwerper Altar", a Flemish carved work, is from the 15th century. The tombstone of Niklas Graf Salm is located in the baptismal chapel.

RUPRECHTSKIRCHE

According to legend, the Ruprechtskirche was founded around 740. It is made of Roman building stones. The holy structure is the oldest in Vienna and was located in the early medieval center of town on a side arm of the Danube, near the Kienmarkt and the Berghof. The essential parts of the building date from the 11th century. The gothic house was documented for the first time in 1161. The smooth, romanesque style and the quadratic tower are still impressive today.

PETERSKIRCHE

Vienna's second-oldest church is only a few steps away from the Pestsäule (Plague-Pillar) in the Graben in Vienna's inner city. It has stood since the 11th century and was built in connection with the Pestsäule and Emperor Leopold I.

The church was made baroque in 1702 and received a copper roof dedicated by Karl VI in 1772. The towers were erected in 1733. The depiction of Emperor Leopold at the entry portal is worth noticing. I. J. M. Rottmayr depicted the ascenion of Mary on the cupola fresco (1713). The baroque altar (1729) shows wooden sculpture by Johann Nepomuk.

NATIONAL OPERA AND OPERA BALL

The Vienna National Opera House, one of the foremost of its kind in the world, was built from 1861–1869 according to plans by August von Siccardsburg and Eduard van der Null, under instructions of Emperor Franz Joseph. At that time it served as Court Opera Theater, opening in 1869 with Mozart's „Don Giovanni". Both builders were so severely criticized, that they were absent from the grand opening. The house was a failure not only in Court but also among the populace because of what was claimed to be a „total lack of style". Hit by a bomb in 1945, the building was totally gutted by fire. It took ten years for

the renovation to be completed by Erich Boltenstern. The reopening took place on November 5, 1955 with Beethoven's „Fidelio" under Director Karl Böhm. The Vienna Philharmonic make up the orchestra of this institution (called the „Staatsoper" since 1919). Its world fame is documented by a long list of important directors such as Richard Strauß, Gustav Mahler, Clemens Kraus, Wilhelm Furtwängler, Herbert v. Karajan, Lorin Maazel, and Claudio Abbado. The Opera House has a capacity for 2209 guests and covers an area of approximately 9000m^2. The orchestra-pit has room for 110 musicians. Two ballet- and three ensemble-

left:
Lotte Tobisch -Labotyn
Organisatorin des Wiener Opernballs

middle:
Placido Domingo

right:
Luciano Pavarotti

practice rooms, a rehearsal stage, 10 solo practice chambers, an organ room and a TV/radio studio with 50 microphone plug-ins are contained in the house. But the Opera House is famous mostly for the world-renowned Vienna Opera Ball.

As far back as 1877, eight years after completion of the pompous building, a special premiere took place – then called „Hofopern-Soiree" (Court-Opera-Soiree). This big event was met with enthusiasm by nobility, as well as by those who could afford such exclusive entertainment. One special detail from those days has been retained up to today: at hardly any other ball in the world is it strictly required that men wear coat and tails (except for those wearing military uniforms). The actual Opera Ball was started in 1935, a bit of old tradition celebrated through interruption and renewal.

During World War Two, performances were interrupted again and again. The first post-war Opera Ball took place on February 2, 1956. For its guests from all over the world, the Vienna Opera Ball is the essence of those events that many of them simply cannot miss out on. It is what made Austria and Vienna famous worldwide.

IMPERIAL THEATRE

Probably the best-known German-language theater is Vienna's Burgtheater, called the „Burg" for short. It is among the oldest and richest in tradition in all the world. In 1741, the „German National Theater" originated on the Michaeler Platz, in an old ballroom in the imperial residence, under approval of Maria Theresia. From 1874–1888 it was moved to the Vienna Ring, into the building it occupies at present, built by Carl Hasenauer and Gottfried Semper. The wide outspreading stairway entrance is especially famous. On account of its Renaissance facade, the building is one of the most interesting along the Vienna Ringstraße. The reliefs depict Apollo and the Muses, which are completed in the picture by over-sized busts of the most celebrated dramatists and poets. From left to right, we see Calderon, Shakespeare, Molière, Goethe, Schiller, Lessing, Halm, Grillparzer and Hebbel.

MUSIC SOCIETY BUILDING

The house „Society of Music-Lovers" in Vienna's 1st district, Dumbastraße 3, was built 1867–69 by Theophil Hansen. The „Musikverein" can be termed the center of Vienna's music life.

The building's great or „golden" room is the setting for the Viennese Philharmonic Orchestra's New Year's concert, which is televised to many countries worldwide. This is the „home" of the celebrated orchestra, although it is open to visiting musicians from all over the globe. Both musicians and listeners enjoy and praise the incomparable acoustics in the room, where concerts are given below golden caryatids. Founded in 1817, the „Society" is in possession of a large music-history collection, including priceless autographs, notes, instruments, and memorabilia. A live concert here is simply a „must" for music lovers.

CITY HALL

Vienna's Rathaus, office of the mayor and community council, was erected in new-gothic style by Friedrich Schmidt from 1872–83. The building is separated somewhat from the Ringstraße by the Rathaus Park. The rich facade is dominated by the towering 98m high central spire, on top of which stands a Vienna landmark, the Rathaus Man, a copper statue 3,4m high. From the Friedrich-Schmidt-Platz at the west entrance, the tour of the Rathaus begins in the Schmidthalle. The banquet hall, the city senate's chamber, the community council's meeting hall, and the tower are accessible, as well as the „Arkadenhof", where summer concerts are regulary held. Rudolf Sieböck planned the Rathaus Park, built in conjunction with the Ringstraße. In it are numerous monuments to artists and politicians, and the traditional „Christkindlmarkt" (christ-child market) is held there before Christmas.

PARLIAMENT

Theophil Hansen created his masterpiece for the Austro-Hungarian monarchy from 1874–1883, the new Reichsrat building, which is now since 1918 the „Parlament", seat of national and federal government. The architecture is reflective of ancient Greece; the pillared porch (porticus) with eight Corinthian columns is clearly inspired from old temple forms. In its gable is a depiction of the Bestowal of the Constitution to the Austrian Peoples by Franz Joseph I. The National Council is seated in the building's north wing, the Federal Council in the south wing. Two mighty ramps, flanked by bronze horse-tamers, lead past marble likenesses of antique historians up to the „porticus". The fountain of Pallas-Athena dominates the space between the two ramps. Carl Kundmann finished the four meter high statue of the „Goddess of Wisdom" in 1902. At her feet tumble the old Austrian river-gods of the Danube, Inn, Elbe, and Moldau.

GRABEN

The Graben, in the heart of the city, is one of Vienna's most distinguished business streets, located next to the Kohlmarkt and the Kärntnerstraße. In the center of the Graben stands the Pestsäule (Plague Pillar), made in 1687 by Bernhard Fischer von Erlach. Leopold I had this pillar erected in memory of the devastation of the plague, which ended in 1679. Both fountains on either side of the Plague Pillar were constructed by Johann Martin Fischer in 1804.

On the corner of the Graben and the Kärntnerstraße is located the „Stock im Eisen" (Stick in the Iron). This is a tree trunk full of hundred of nails, which was supposedly crafted as a masterpiece by a locksmith with the aid of the devil. The name „Graben" („moat") comes from the fortress moat which was located on this site from Roman times until the mid 12th century.

HAAS HOUSE

Across from St. Stephan's cathedral, on the corner of the Graben and Stephansplatz, stands the Haas House. This very original building designed by Viennese architect Hans Hollein is the source of much discussion. Some people find the shiny chrome and glass building interesting and beautiful, and are of the opinion that contemporary architecture does indeed belong in the inner city. On the other hand, some critics find the structure vain, tas-teless, overdone and gaudy. The Haas House opened in September 1990. World-renowned fashion designers and cosmetic firms are established in the seven-story building. Visitors can treat themselves to fine cuisine in the luxurious cafe and restaurant. Following his obsession, Hollein designed and shaped every detail of his building, down to the last square meter.

JUGENDSTIL IN VIENNA

In the Jugendstil epoch, many important buildings were erected in Vienna. One of the best-known is the Secession on the Getreidemarkt, near the Naschmarkt. In 1897, active Viennese artists completed the separation from the „isms" of academic tradition and founded the „Vienna Secession". The initiators of this movement were, among others, Josef Hoffman, Gustav Klimt, Joseph Maria Olbrich and Otto Wagner. Joseph Maria Olbrich, a student of Hasenauer and Otto Wagner, built the exhibition-building – called Secession for short – for this group in 1897–98. Gustav Klimt designed the no longer remaining metal doors. The cubic construction is decorated with gold-plated iron laurel branches. In spite of the interior changes made in 1964, the outer form has remained original up to today. The motto, „Der Zeit ihre Kunst, der Kunst ihre Freiheit" („To time its own art, to art its own freedom"), is written above the entry to this temple of art. Two houses on the Linke Wienzeile are from this period. The Linke Wienzeile was originally supposed to be an elegant boulevard leading from the Hofburg

above:
Majolika-House

below left:
Secession, an exhibition by important artists

LOOS HOUSE

The Looshaus, named after its builder, the Jugendstil architect Adolf Loos, was constructed in 1910. The house was erected for a men's fashion firm as an apartment- and office-building, and had such a daring facade that public reaction caused construction to be temporarily shut down. Loos and his ideas cleared the way for a new, objective method of building. He was the chief architect for the office of housing develpoment in Vienna from 1920–1922.

all the way to Schönbrunn. Otto Wagner (1841–1918), the great city planner in Vienna at the turn of the century, built both these houses in 1898.

He paid the construction costs partially out of his own pocket to stress his demand for polychromatic facades. House number 38 had its facade bearing floral ornamentation (see illustration p. 60, above right). Further examples of Wagner's great architecture are located on the Karlsplatz (subway station) and along the suburban and urban rail lines.

NATIONAL LIBRARY

The former „Hofbibliothek" on the Josefsplatz was completed (according to plans by Johann Bernhard Fischer von Erlach) by his son Joseph Emanuel between 1723 and 1735. The stateroom is one of the greatest spacial creations of the late baroque era. Daniel Gran made the magnificent frescoes. The allegories of various sciences are found in the cupola, and on the ceiling is a depiction of Karl VI. The National Library contains an inestimably valuable collection of more than 2.2 million handwritten and printed works, precious leatherbound volumes from the estate of Prince Eugen, as well as numerous maps and notebooks.

HUNDERT
WASSER

HUNDERTWASSER HOUSE

The „Hundertwasserhaus", built by and named after Friedensreich Hundertwasser, is another object of interest. It stands in the Löwengasse in the 3rd district. Friedensreich Hundertwasser, one of the most important contemporary Viennese painters and academic professor, realized a dream of ecological living in the construction of this dwelling. The painter has an invincible aversion to geometric lines. The Viennese community had the house built, and it was finished in 1985. Bricks and wood, but no plastics, were used in the construction. The „irregularities" in the form of the house were added by the artist during the building procedure. Thousands have visited this unique structure, mostly viewing it from the outside, out of respect for it inhabitants.

MUSEUM OF ART HISTORY

The Museum of Art History houses the most important painting collection in the world as well as an extensive collection of sculpture and arts and crafts, an Egyptian collection with numerous mummies, collections of Greek and Etruscan artworks, a coin cabinet and the Ambraser portrait collection.

It was built to plans by Carl Hasenauer and Gottfried Semper between 1871 and 1888. Its rich inner design is a collaboration of re-

Entrance to the Museum of Art History

nowned artists such as Hans Makart, Gustav and Ernst Klimt and August Eisenmenger. The collections come from Vienna, Ambras (Tyrol), Graz, Innsbruck, Brussels and Prague. They were brought together into today's museum-building in 1889. Through purchases, donations and excavation finds, the total amassment in the museum totals 480,000 pieces.

One of the most valuable and most extensive of the collections is that of the paintings of Pieter Breughel. Furthermore, the gallery owns masterpieces by Raffael, Rembrandt, van Eyck, Lukas Cranach, Holbein, Dürer, Velasquez, Titian, Rubens and many other great masters.

Brueghel the Elder: Peasants' Dance

above left:
Rubens, Peter Paul: Helene Fourment,
the artist's second wife ("The Fur"),
circa 1638

right side:
Raffael: Madonna in the Greenery

below left:
Rembrandt: Titius

MUSEUM OF NATURAL HISTORY

The Museum of Natural History belongs to the „Kaiserforum" (Emperor's Forum) consisting of the Hofburg, the Neue Burg and the Museums, and is next to the Museum of Art History. Gottfried Semper planned this Forum, and Carl Hasenauer was the Museum of Natural History's interior architect.

The ground floor of the museum was once filled with the private collection of Karl I, husband of Maria Theresia. Franz Joseph I enlarged the collection greatly.

Today the museum has eight departments. The mineralogical-petrographic department, with its collection of meteorites, is the largest and oldest in the world. Fossil remains of plants and animals from pre-human times are featured in the geological-paleontological department. The prehistoric department concerns itself with human life, presenting finds from the Hallstadt age, as well as the „Venus of Willendorf".

Visitors can examine the development and biological history of mankind in the anthropological department.

The botanical department, with the collection „Vienna Herbarium", three zoological departments (vertebrates, invertebrates and insects) and a petting zoo for children are located on the second floor of the museum.

above left: Reptile Room
above right: Meteorite Room

middle: Grey Peacockpheasant
below: Dinosaur Room

left side: Hofburg (areal view)

NEW HOFBURG

With its 18 wings, 54 stairways, 19 court-yards and roughly 2600 rooms, the Hofburg is the secular center of Vienna. It was the Emperor's home until 1918. The building complex today houses numerous museums and collections, the Spanish Riding School and the Austrian National Library. In the Leopoldinischen Wing are found the Federal President's offices. The Hofburg is a complex which experienced many expansions in the course of centuries, and for this reason there are juxtaposed many different architectural styles. Defense installations began in 1275 under Bohemian King Ottokar and were completed under Rudolf II of Habsburg. Following tradition, every ruler built his own apartments, not using those of his predecessors, in order to

enlarge the Hofburg. In 1515, the first „Wiener Kongress" was centered in the Hofburg. The second „Wiener Kongress", which lasted nine months, was one of the flashiest events ever occurring at the Hofburg – it is said that there was more dancing than discussing. Even today, elegant balls are held in the masquerade rooms.

The Neue (new) Burg was erected in 1908 under Franz Joseph I, separating the Burggarten from the Heldenplatz. The twenty figures on the facade represent the main epochs of Austrian history. The Museum of Ethnology is located here as well as the largest weapon collection in the world, a collection of old musical instruments and the Museum of Austrian Culture.

above: Hofburg inner courtyard

above right:
Emperor Franz Joseph I.'s study

below right:
a view of the Wiener Hofburg's dining room

Leaving the Heldenplatz and walking in the direction of the Alte (old) Burg, one comes to the square „In der Burg", the Burg's inner courtyard, built for Emperor Maximilian II as a tournament-ground. Here is located the monument to Franz I, represented as the Imperator Augustus, with the inscription „amorem meum populis meis" meaning „My love for my peoples". The oldest part of the Hofburg is called the Schweizerhof (Swiss Court), because the Swiss Guard was stationed there in Maria Theresia's time. The Burgkapelle (chapel) is the only example of gothic style remaining in the Hofburg, being mentioned as early as 1296 but remodeled in 1449. The Stallburg is from the 16th century, and is still used by the Spanish

Riding School to house their Lipizzans. In the Imperial Chancellery Wing were located the work- and living rooms of Emperor Franz Joseph and those of Empress Elisabeth in the Amalien Wing. In the table- and silver chamber, the so-called „tableware of Milan" is presented, a gold-plated silver service 30m long which is enough for 140 dinner guests.

An essential part of the Hofburg is the Schatzkammer (treasure-chamber). This magnificent and beautiful collection originated in 1533 with Emperor Ferdinand I's Kunstkammer (artchamber), and has been enriched through the years with many art pieces from Habsburg collections. The complicated lock of the entryway door bears the initials of Karl VI, who

Crown of Emperor Rudolf II: "Habsburgerkrone"

Imperial crown of the Holy Roman Empire

placed the treasures in the ground floor of the old Burg in 1712. The collection is separated into an ecclesiastical and a secular department. The crown jewels of the Holy Roman Empire and the Imperial crown are main attractions. Also presented are the 4th century agate bowl honored as the holy grail, Maria Theresia's jewels, knightly ornaments from the Order of Golden Fleece, the insignia of the Austrian archdukes and many other precious stones. Included are Winterhalter's portraits of Franz Joseph I and Elisabeth, painted in 1865. The

The King of Rome's throne cradle

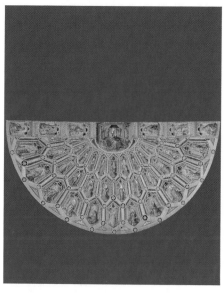

The burgundian mass-robe of the order of the golden fleece

Coronationgarments of the Lombardo-Venetian Kingdom

Burgundian court cup

„Heilige Römische Reich Deutscher Nation" (Holy Roman Empire of the German Nation) was officially called „Imperium Romanum", or „Imperium Sacrum" („Roman Empire" or „Holy Empire"), and saw itself as an ideological and political continuation of the Roman Empire.

With the Pope's crowning of Charlemagne in 800, this idea was realized without gaining legal importance. The German King was chosen by electors. With the exception of the Wittelsbacher Karl VII (1742–1745), only Habsburgers wore the imperial crown.

Hyacinth "La Bella"

Chain of the Golden Fleece

THE HOUSE OF HABSBURG

The Habsburgs shaped Austrian history from the 13th century until 1918. Their ancestral home, the Habichtsburg, is located in the Swiss canton Aargau on the Wülpelsberg, and was built in 1028. The Habsburgs' hereditary rule of Austria was claimed in the 13th century. Rudolf I of Habsburg gave the duchies of Austria and Styria to his sons at the end of the 13th century, and Habsburg rule continued (with some interruptions) up until our own century. The last Austrian emperor, Karl I, abdicated in 1918. Probably the most famous Habsburg

was Franz Joseph I. He came to the throne as an 18-year-old in 1848, and ruled until his death in 1916. In 1854 he married the Bavarian Princess Elisabeth, daughter of Duke Maximilian of Bavaria, in Vienna's Augustine Church. Sisi, as the empress was lovingly nicknamed, could not cope with the strict Viennese court life (based on Spanish court ceremony), and she became more and more a recluse, known for her restless journeys in later years.

SPANISH RIDING SCHOOL

The „Winterreitschule" (Winter Riding School) was completed in 1735 by Joseph Fischer von Erlach. It is located between the Schweizerhof and the Stallburg. The magnificent baroque Große Saal (Great Hall) and the gallery with 16 Corinthian columns was the scene of numerous festivals at the time of the Wiener Kongreß. Today the „Spanische Hofreitschule" offers demonstrations of the classical art of riding unique to Vienna. The riders wear historical uniforms. Karl VI, who bred intelligent, noble horses at the stud farm „Lipizza" in what is now Yugoslavia, east of Triest, founded the school. Besides being so intelligent, the Lipizzans are also remarkable in that they are black as foals, then white as full-grown horses. The Lipizzans are a cross between Andalusian, Arabian, and Napolitan breeds. They were good not only in battle but also in horse-ballett, and in pulling Franz Joseph's carriage. Today these unique horses are bred in the federal stud farm Piber, near Köflach in Styria. Public shows are given Wednesdays, from March to June and from September to November.

Gold cabinet in the Lower Belvedere

BELVEDERE

Schloß Belvedere is one of the most famous baroque palaces. Prince Eugen von Savoyen, the „sword of the Habsburgs" and conqueror of the Turks, had this summer residence erected. The building, constructed by Johann Lukas von Hildebrand, consists of two places. The Bavarian Dominique Girard made the magnificent garden.

In 1725 the complex was essentially finished. The upper Belvedere served as reception, and the lower was Prince Eugen's summer dwelling.

After his death, Belvedere was given to the Habsburgs. Joseph II brought the imperial painting collection to Belvedere in 1777. In 1806, the Schloß Ambras collection (from Tyrol, which had become Bavarian under Napoleon) was added. These collections were brought to the newly built Museum of Art History (on the Vienna Ringstraße) in 1890. Successor to the throne Franz Ferdinand resided briefly in the upper Belvedere after 1894. He was later assassinated in Sarajevo. The famous composer Anton Bruckner lived in the neighboring custodian wing until his death in 1896. Belvedere was the scene of a great Austrian historical event on May 15, 1955. On that day, the Austrian National Contract (Staatsvertrag) was signed in the great marble hall of the upper Belvedere.

The occupation of Austria by the victorious powers of World War Two was now over, and Austria was free again. Today, Belvedere is part of the Austrian Gallery. The lower Belvedere houses the Austrian Baroque Museum, among other things, exhibiting sculpture and painting from the 17th and 18th centuries. In the „Orangerie" of the lower Belvedere is located the Museum of Austrian Medieval Art, where works from the 12th to the 16th century are shown. The gallery of the 19th and 20th centuries is in the upper Belvedere, with departments for classicism, Biedermeier, the Ring-straßen Era, Jugendstil, and the largest collection of Klimt, Schiele, and Kokoschka. On summer evenings in the upper Belvedere park, performances of „Son et Lumiere" are shown, which detail the history of the building.

Gustav Klimt: "The Kiss" exhibited in the Austrian Gallery

JUGENDSTIL IN VIENNA

In the Jugendstil epoch, many important buildings were erected in Vienna. One of the best-known is the Secession on the Getreidemarkt, near the Naschmarkt. In 1897, active Viennese artists completed the separation from the „isms" of academic tradition and founded the „Vienna Secession". The initiators of this movement were, among others, Josef Hoffman, Gustav Klimt, Joseph Maria Olbrich and Otto Wagner. Joseph Maria Olbrich, a student of Hasenauer and Otto Wagner, built the exhibition-building – called Secession for short – for this group in 1897–98. Gustav Klimt designed the no longer remaining metal doors. The cubic construction is decorated with gold-plated iron laurel branches. In spite of the interior changes made in 1964, the outer form has remained original up to today. The motto, „Der Zeit ihre Kunst, der Kunst ihre Freiheit" („To time its own art, to art its own freedom"), is written above the entry to this temple of art. Two houses on the Linke Wienzeile are from this period. The Linke Wienzeile was originally supposed to be an elegant boulevard leading from the Hofburg all the way to Schönbrunn. Otto Wagner (1841–1918), the great city planner in Vienna at the turn of the century, built both these houses in 1898. He paid the construction costs partially out of his own pocket to stress his demand for polychromatic facades. House number 38 had its facade bearing floral ornamentation (see illustration p. 60, above right). Further examples of Wagner's great architecture are located on the Karlsplatz (subway station) and along the suburban and urban rail lines.

Exhibition: Michelangelo Pistoletto: "Oggetti in Meno" 26.1. - 25.2.1990

above: Exhibition "Umweg Moderne Modern Detour" 19.10 - 2.12.1990
below left: Exhibition "Viennese Furniture" 7.6. - 16.7.1989
below right: Egon Schiele: Poster: "The Round Table" for the 49th exhibition, 1918

ALBERTINA

The biggest and most important collection of graphic works is in the Albertina, which has around 50,000 drawings and over a million graphic and printed works.

These works offer an almost continuous overview of international art from the 15th to the 20th century, including such artists as Raffael, Michelangelo, Dürer, Rembrandt and Rubens. The Albertina is located in the baroque Palais Taroucca, which was remodeled from 1801 to 1804 for Maria Theresia's son-in-law, Duke Albert von Sachsen-Teschen. Fundamental to the Albertina are the collection of drawings and works of Duke Albert and the collection of copper engravings from the imperial court library and formerly in the possession of Prince Eugen von Savoyen.

The name „Albertina" was coined in 1873 by director Moritz von Thausing, in commemoration of its founder on the occasion of the Vienna World's Fair.

right:
Egon Schiele: Male nude, left profile, self portrait (1910)

left:
Albrecht Dürer:
Self-portrait as 13-year-old (1484)

55

Michelangelo: Nude Boy

Rudolf von Alt: The "Am Hof" Square in Vienna, 1892

A. Renoir: "River Landscape"

TECHNICAL MUSEUM

Near Schönbrunn in the 14th district lies the Technical Museum, built between 1909 and 1913 by Hans Schneider and opened in 1918. The first exhibited pieces in the three-story building belonged to the imperial physics cabinet. Some of the most interesting objects and presentations include the show-clock with planetarium (1555), James Watt's steam engine (1790), models of Ressel's shipscrew (1829), a reproduced coal mine, Mitterhofer's typewriter (1864), models of W. Kress' airplane (he built the first seaplane) and models of Lilienthal's glider. The railroad museum and the post-and-telegraph museum are further departments. The first sewing machine by Josef Madersperger (1815) and the first gasoline-powered car by Siegfried Marcus (1875) are doubtless special attractions.

Steam locomotives "Ajax" (1841) and "Steinbrück" (1848)

Empress Elisabeth's carriage, built in 1873

above:	*model of a violin-maker's workshop, 19th century*
middle left:	*Etrich-II "Dove", built 1909/10 - Prototype of all "Dove constructions"*
middle right:	*miraculous automatic writing machine by Friedrich Knaus from the year 1760*
below left:	*postal tube system by Felbinger, 1890 used in Vienna until 1956*
below right:	*Typewriter by Peter Mitterhofer, Vienna model, 1864*

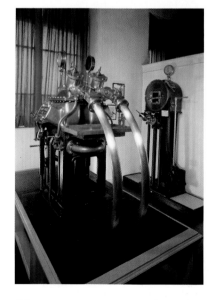

above left: Lohner-Porsche electromobile, 1900 model, built by the "Vienna k. u. k. Court Wagon and Automobile factory Jacob Lohner & Co".

above right: Steyr 50, called the "Steyr Baby". A total of 13,000 were built from 1937 to 1940.

middle: Austro-Daimler 6/25 HP with four cylinder motor, 1920, constructed by Ferdinand Porsche.

below:" Silver Arrow", Mercedes-Benz 2.5 liter formula racecar, type W 196 with streamlined chassis, 1955

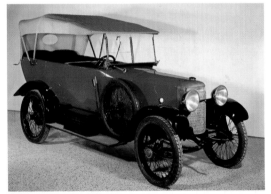

MUSICIANS IN VIENNA

Many famous musicians lived and worked in the music capital Vienna, such as Johann Strauß, Wolfgang Amadeus Mozart, Gustav Mahler, Ludwig van Beethoven, Franz Schubert, Joseph Haydn and Anton Bruckner, who all contributed to Vienna's worldwide celebrity. Many of them ara commemorated in monuments.

In 1886 Viktor Tilgner created the Mozart monument which has stood in the Burggarten since the end of World War Two. And in Mozart's honor, 1991 has been declared „Mozart-Year".

Caspar Zumbusch's bronze statue of Beethoven was made in 1880 during the general shaping of the Ringstraße.

left: *W. A. Mozart, painted by D. Krafft (exhibited in the house of "The society of Music-lovers")*

below left: *Mozart's signature*

below right: *L. v. Beethoven, oilpainting by J. W. Mähler, 1804 - 05 (exhibited in the Pasqualati-House, Vienna 1st district, Mölkerbastei 8)*

Johann Strauß, born in Vienna in 1825 and cofounder of the „Golden Age of Operetta", composed 496 great works in his life, for example the „Blue Danube" waltz, the operet-tas „Die Fledermaus" and „Der Zigeunerba-ron".His monument stands in the Vienna City Park.

Franz Schubert, painted by W. A. Rieder, 1825 (exhibited in the Schubert-Museum, Vienna 9th district, Nußdorfer Str. 54)

CLOCK MUSEUM

The Clock Museum in the Schulhof in the 1st district contains roughly 3500 different clocks, of which 1000 are exhibited. Three floors house a collection which shows the developement of the mechanical clock from its origins up to the modern quartz clock. The museum was founded through the private initiative of the schoolteacher Rudolf Kaftan, who received the building in 1917 from the city of Vienna, to house his expansive private collection. In that same year, 270 pocketwatches were purchased from Marie von Ebner-Eschenbach. Today, the largest item is a heavy tower clock from St. Stephan's cathedral. The most expansive piece in the collection is a baroque grandfather's clock from the court monastery. A tiny grandfather's clock the size of a thimble is the smallest item in the exhibit.

"Onion" Clock, circa 1770, Isaac Robus, London

Ankeruhr am Hohen Markt

Model of a fire truck equipped for smoke and suffocation danger, 1833

FIRE DEPARTMENT MUSEUM

The Fire Department Museum, located „Am Hof" in the 1st district, was founded in 1970. On the occasion of the 300th anniversary of the Vienna Fire Department, the museum was completely renovated.

Nine show rooms contain exhibits of diverse items of interest relating to the fire department, including the evolution of respiratory-protection devices, telegraphs (among others, the steepler of St. Stephan), an old-fashioned switchboard (which was in use until 1989), fire fighters' clothing and protective suits, and depictions of the fire department in action at such spectacular

fires as that of the Ring Theater at the end of the 19th century or that of the Gerngross Department Store in the Mariahilferstraße recently, or the Steyr Central Offices Fire on the Ring. 27 antique automobiles reflect the fire department's vehicular history.

A video at the museum's entrance sets the mood for visitors. Tours can be pre-arranged by telephone with the Fire Department (groups of 7 or more), mainly on weekdays. The museum is open on Sundays and holidays. The doorman can give more information.

FIAKER MUSEUM

The Fiaker, the taxi of the previous century, continues to decorate the city, and a museum in the 17th district is dedicated to its preservation.

Founded in the early 1960's, the museum contains as many as 3000 models and different carriages, as well as flags, horse taxometers, memorabilia and a historical display of the Fiaker Ball. In order to see the Fiaker carriages „live in action", one must seek out their various parking spots in the city, where passersby are invited to a ride.

The Fiaker Museum's picture-gallery includes potraits of Vienna's most famous Fiaker coachman, „Bratfisch", whose celebrity derives from a tragic incident: it was he who drove Crown Prince Rudolf (son of Emperor Franz Joseph and Empress Sisy) on what was to be Rudolf's last journey to Mayerling, where he and Baroness Mary Vetsera met their doom.

The name „Fiaker" originates in the Rue Saint Fiacre in Paris, where coaches for hire stood parked outside of an inn bearing the portrait of Saint Fiacrius, an Irish monk.

Nicole Sauvage had introduced these carriages in around 1650, and soon afterwards most large European cities (Vienna, Berlin, Brussels, Hamburg, Leipzig, Dresden etc.) had their own „Fiakers". The first Fiaker license in Austria was granted in 1693 under the rule of Emperor Leopold I. Located in the Fiaker House (built in 1852) in the former „Fiaker-gass'n" or Fiaker Road, now named Veronikagasse, the Fiaker Museum can be visited free of charge every first Wednesday of the month or by special appointment.

ARSENAL

The Arsenal (in which the Museum of Military History is located) was built in 1849 as an arsenal-and-barracks group, a fortress against attacks by armed revolutionaries. The original complex of buildings had an area of 690 by 480 m. The Arsenal was planned in the style of the buildings on the Ringstraße by Theophil Hansen, Ludwig Förster, Eduard van der Nüll, Carl Rösner and August Siccard von Siccardsburg. In the remaining parts of this structure are found the museum's „Hall of Fame" and „Generals' Hall". Among the countless exhibits are models of the k. and k. navy, weapon collections from the times of Maria Theresia, and the „Sarajevo" room, where the automobile and blood-stained uniform of Franz Ferdinand, assassinated successor to the throne, are shown.

Helmet of the first imperial and royal Guard

Renè Magritte: "The Voice of Blood", 1959

MODERN ART

The Museum of Modern Art, open since 1979, is located in the Gartenpalais Liechtenstein. International art from the 1960's and -70's, including Pop-Art, as well as Photographic Realism and Nouveau Realisme, are represented here. 20th century Austrian art, from Jugendstil to the present, completes the diverse collection. Modern art in baroque surroundings – an exciting contrast!

68

Waldmüller: "Young Lady at her toilet"

HISTORICAL MUSEUM OF THE CITY OF VIENNA

The Historical Museum of the City of Vienna, founded in the 19th century, was located in the new city hall until 1943. The present museum building on Vienna's Karlsplatz was designed by the architect Oswald Haerdtl, a colleague of Josef Hoffmann. It opened in 1959. Complete with cultural-historical collections, the museum offers a journey through Vienna's past.

STREETCAR MUSEUM

Vienna's municipal public transportation system has produced quite a variety of vehicles and equipment in its more than 100-year history.

Not only the tramway-fan but also the layman or expert interested in history and technical progress can learn from the past. The Vienna Streetcar Museum was created in this spirit. Located at the Erdberg switching station in the 3rd district, the museum was opened in May of 1986.

Presently, the museum is contained in four large rooms. In 1992, the museum's construction will be finished, and in its final form the museum will have room for approximately 100 streetcars and buses from the public transportation sys-

tem. The exhibited vehicles are partly the property of the Vienna City Works-Public Transportation System, the Technical Museum, and primarily the „Vienna Tramway Museum Club" and the „Society of Railroad Friends".

Reconstruction work on the vehicles is done according to strict standards, with original blueprints and documents and photographs of original vehicles being used for the exact replication of antique items.

Even original tools are used, as far as possible. Most of the vehicles are in working order, and on special nostalgic rides, they are brought out of the museum onto the streets. The museum is open from the end of May until the end of October on weekends and holidays.

AUSTRIAN TABACCO MUSEUM

The Austrian Tabacco Museum in the Messepalast (Mariahilferstraße entrance) with its 4000 exhibits documents an extraordinary, four-century chapter of Austrian and foreign cultural history.

The collection belongs to Austria-Tabak, the Austrian tabacco industry. The long-vanished world of smoking and snuffing as an expression of cultivation, especially among 18th century nobility, awaits the visitor. Pipes of clay, wood, porcellan and meerschaum, snuff boxes inlaid with jewels, gold, silver, half-gems and enamel, cigar and cigarette cases as well as paintings, documents and historical advertisement material illustrate the changing history of the tobacco museum from its origins to the present. The Austrian Tabacco Museum is closed on Mondays. Opening hours are: Tuesday 10 AM to 7 PM, Wednesday and Friday from 10 AM to 3 PM and Saturday and Sunday from 9 AM to 1 PM.

Georg Ferdinand Waldmüller: "The Pipe-dealer in the Coffee-House", 1824

SCHÖNBRUNN

Schloß Schönbrunn is one of the best-known and most representative architectural structures of Vienna. Emperor Matthias discovered a „Schönnen Brunnen" („beautiful fountain") while hunting in what are now the grounds around the palace, after which he named the later built Schönbrunn, and which supplied it with water until the end of the 18th century. At that time the area was covered with a thick forest, full of game. Originally, the „Katter-mühle" (Katter mill) stood here, first mentioned in 1311, and in 1271 a little castle, the „Katterburg", was built. Maximilian II took possession in 1568 and had the building turned into a hunting palace. The famous Schönbrunner Tiergarten (zoo) was built under his orders. After the Turks destroyed the hunting palace, Johann Bernhard Fischer von Erlach drew plans for a magnificent building under instructions from Leopold I from 1692–1693, with ambitions to

surpass the French Versailles in beauty. This was at first meant to stand on the location of today's Gloriette Hill, but for financial reasons a simpler building was constructed and finished in 1700. Joseph I enjoyed staying there, but his son Karl VI neglected further construction. Finally, under Maria Theresia, Schönbrunn was completed 1744–1749 in rococo style by Nicolaus Pacassi. Jean Trehet designed the beautiful French-style park grounds in 1705–1706. The park received its modern form from Johann Ferdinand Hetzendorf von Hohenberg and Adrian van Steckhoven from 1753 to 1775. With its trimmed walls of trees, alleyways, flowers, lawn-beds and fountains it is one of Europe's most beautiful parks. Since Maria Theresia's time, Schönbrunn has been second preference only to the Hofburg as residence for the Holy Roman and later the Austrian Emperors.

The palace has 1441 rooms and halls. 390 of these were actually used by the Court for living and receiving guests. 139 kitchens cooked for almost 1000 people. The Great Gallery, also called the Rittersaal, was used as a reception and festival hall. The frescoes in the Rittersaal are by Gregorio Guglielmi in homage to Maria Theresia.

With an area of 1,76 km2 Schönnbrunn was comparatively four times bigger than the Vatican. Napoleon's only son, the Duke of Reichstadt, lived and died here. In 1830 the later Emperor Franz Joseph I was born in Schönbrunn. Karl I, the last Austrian emperor, abdicated here in 1918. During World War II, the entire palace and grounds suffered heavy damages, but repairs were finished in 1952. Today, governmental receptions take place in the staterooms.

above: Millions Room
below: Great Gallery

The palatial park has an area of 197 acres. The Neptune fountain, the obelisk and the Roman ruins are especially worth seeing. The park stretches out to the Gloriette, built by Johann Ferdinand Hetzendorf von Hohenberg and is bordered by Roman trophies. The open pillared wall is 19m high and 95m long. One of the most beautiful views of Vienna is to be seen from the terrace of the Gloriette.

above:
Chinese Cabinet

below:
Bergl-Room

above:
Court Theater

below:
Blue Chinese Salon

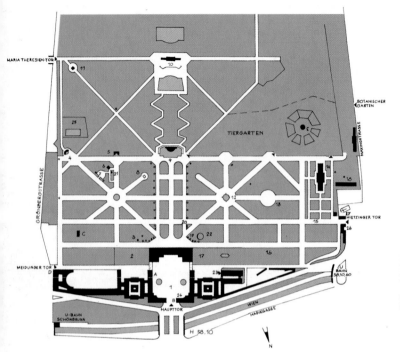

WAGENBURG

The Wagenburg is located in the former Winterreitschule (Winter Riding School), one building east of the palace. It is the home of one of the world's largest collections of historical decorative and practical wagons. Exhibit- pieces from 1690–1918 can be seen. The showpiece of the display is the imperial wagon, the state carriage of the Vienna Court. Sedan chairs, sleds, bicycles and automobiles are included in the collection.

Imperial Carriage

PALM HOUSE

One of Schönbrunn's special attractions is the Palm House. Built in 1883 by Ferdinand Hetzendorf von Hohenberg, it houses tropical plants such as orchids, palms and even carniphagous plants. To the visitor the Palm House offers a magnificient variety of colours usually only to be found in tropical regions.

BUTTERFLY HOUSE

In the Sundial House in Schönbrunn, Austria's first tropical butterfly house is established. Roughly 200 tropical butterflies of 25 different species have a home here. The room temperature of 28 degrees Celsius and 85 percent humidity recreate the natural habitat of the animals, and they move freely within the rooms. Species representation varies with the seasons. The butterflies come partly from Thailand and Costa Rica, and are delivered as pupae. Some butterflies are bred here in the butterfly house.

ZOO

The Tiergarten, an essential part of Schönbrunn, was finished in 1759. The central pavilion was once the imperial couple's prefered recreational spot in summer. Around it are grouped twelve animal-houses. Today the zoo is a favorite among places to go.

middle: Attacus Atlas

79

PRATER

Vienna's Prater, the huge recreational area, goes back as far as 1403. Under Ferdinand I, the chestnut alleyway was planted in 1537. After Emperor Joseph II opened the former imperial hunting grounds in the Prater meadows to the public in 1766, the area developed into a favorite relaxation place for Viennese. At this time, the first stands, restaurants and coffee houses appeared, and the „Wurstelprater" („sausage Prater") or Volksprater was born.

Further attractions, such as merry-go-rounds, bowling alleys, carousels and fireworks followed. Montgolfiere's Balloons took off here in 1791. In 1840, Basilio Calafati set up his famous „Great Chinese" carousel on what is now the „Calafati Platz". Kasperl, the main character in puppet shows, has had many hairraising adventures here, too.

The World's Fair took place on the Prater grounds in 1873. Exhibition halls built at that time exist today to some extent and are used by the Vienna Fair. The Englishman Basset built the 430-ton and 645m high steel Riesenrad (Giant Wheel) in 1896–97, giving Vienna its world-renowned landmark.

SPASS FÜR ALLE

DANUBE TOWER

No sight-seeing tour of Vienna is complete without a visit to the Danube Tower. It was erected for the Donaupark (Danube Park) within the framework of preparatory work for the International Garden Show in 1964. 252 m high, the tower was built by architect Hannes Lintl and statics expert Dr. Robert Krapfenbauer. An observation deck is located at a heigh of 150 m, from which a view of all Vienna and its surroundings and as far out as the Austrian mountain country is possible (the weather permitting). Above this deck is a slowly revolving restaurant, which allows the observer a changing viewpoint. Next to this culinarily superb restaurant is the Danube Tower's Viennese coffee house, often visited for a „chat over coffee", similar to the English „5 o'clock tea", only less formal. The observation deck, restaurant and coffee house can be reached in a matter of seconds by means of an elevator built within the tower. The wonderful Danube Park has an area of 1 km2 and lies between the Old and the New Danube, and is a frequently visited recreational spot, dominated by the Danube Tower. The park is easily accessible by subway or by car. The tower and the park are near the Uno-City and the Danube Island, another recreational area.

UNO CITY

In 1979 the United Nations made Vienna its third official headquarters, next to New York and Geneva. The Viennese regard this Uno-City, called Vienna International Center, as a separate city in itself. It was built from 1973–79 by Johann Staber. The mighty construction is made primarily of glass, steel and cement. The glass facades with a total of 24,000 windows make the buildings paritcularly striking. Around 3800 UNO employees from more than 100 countries work here. Several international organizations, such as the International Atomic Energy Organization, the United Nations Industrial Development Organization, the UN Welfare Organization for Palestine, the Department for International Trade and the UN Narcotics Commission are headquartered here. Employees can shop „duty-free" in the UNO-city, and Austrian work holidays are not observed. Austria entered this world organization in 1955.

KAHLENBERG

The Kahlenberg is a favorite place for outings in Vienna. The Order of the Kamaldulenser founded a heritage on the uninhabited mountain in 1629, which was destroyed by the Turks in 1683. Today the baroque Josefskirche stands on the site. There is a copy of the „Schwarze Madonna" („black madonna") of Tschenstochau kept in the church, which is a memorial to Poland's contribution to the defeat over the Turks, as is the Sobieskikapelle (Sobieski Chapel). The Stephaninenwarte or -lookout and a television broadcaster are located on the 484 m high summit. A restaurant next to the church is open to visitors.

Vienna Panorama

LEOPOLDSBERG

The Leopoldsberg is one of the last elevations of the Vienna Woods – and therefore also of the Alps. St. Markgraf Leopold III erected the „Babenbergerburg", with a chapel to St. Georg, on the Leopoldsberg in the 12th century. The Burg and the chapel were destroyed in 1529 by the Turks. Emperor Lepold I began building a new church on the site in 1679. The „Historic Mass" before the victorious battle against the Turks was held in 1683 within its unfinished walls. The church was finished in 1693 and dedicated to St. Leopold, whose name was given to the mountain.

VIENNESE HOSPITALITY VIENNESE GUESTS

VIENNA, THE METROPOLIS FOR EVERYONE

There's something for everyone in Vienna, the metropolis in the heart of Europe. Whether you are a lover of culture and the arts, an avid museum-goer, or simply curious to explore the city's entertainment and shopping opportunities, you're sure to find what you're looking for. „Vienna is always in season", as the saying goes, and the city has much to offer the whole year round. Each season has its unique array of atmosphere and events. Vienna blooms in the spring, with its numerous outdoor gardens decorating the streets and inviting guests to relax with food and drink. Among Vienna's many spring events are the Haydn Days, the Vienna Spring Marathon and the Vienna Fair, which take place in March, as well as the Days of Sacred Music at the beginning of April. May and June are highlighted by the Vienna City Festival, the Prater Spring Festival and the Vienna Festival Weeks. Spring is the ideal time to get acquainted with the city and its surroundings. In the hot summer months, the night life dominates the scene. During the day, most people spend their time in the many municipal swimming pools or on the Danube Island, which receives between 100 and 200 thousand guests each summer weekend. Approximately 45 recreational facilities such as surfing and diving schools, water ski-lifts and bicycle rentals are available for those seeking outdoor activity. And the Prater amusement park is in full swing during the summer until the end of August or mid-September.

The outdoor gardens and the ice cream parlors close up gradually in autumn, to be replaced by chestnut-roasters on many city street-corners. As the leaves change colors and start to fall, the main season for city tourism begins. Many visitors use the autumn season for cultural education, going to museums and exhibitions and viewing architectural monuments. Sometimes in early November, the city may be covered with a thin snowfall, which however usually disappears as quickly as it came. Although Vienna is somewhat quieter in winter, the shopping days before Christmas bring hectic life to the streets. Vienna is famous for its annual Christ Child Market in front of the City Hall. Another special winter event is the Vienna Philharmonic New Year's Concert at the Music Society, which is televised worldwide.

IMPORTANT EVENTS

Vienna offers numerous events all year round, some of which are listed here, taking place annually with little variation in appointed date and time.

JANUARY:
- Vienna Philharmonic New Year's Concert (January 1)
- Various New Year's Eve Balls
- Emperor's Ball (Kaiserball)

- Flower Ball (Blumenball)
- Vienna Philharmonic Ball
- Vienna Medical Doctor's Ball
- Mass with Vienna's Sängerknaben (Boys' Choir) (September – June)

FEBRUARY:
- Numerous balls, including the famous Vienna Opera Ball
- Masked Ball at Vienna's Imperial Court

- Bonbon Ball
- Vienna Coffeeboilers' Ball
- Lawyers' Ball
- Rudolfiner Masquerade, Carnival Parade

MARCH:
- Haydn Days
- Vienna Spring Marathon
- Dance Week
- Viennale Film Festival
- Vienna Fair
- Spanish Riding School Show
  (March – June)

APRIL:
- Days of Sacred Music
- Waltz and Operetta concerts
  (April – October)
- Sightseeing tours with the Danube Steamship Company (April – October)

MAY:
- Prater Spring Festival
- Vienna Festival Weeks (May and June)
- City Festival

JUNE:
- Prater Flower Parade
- Concordia Ball

JULY:
- Spectaculum
- Vienna Music Summer (July and August)
- International Youth Festival
- Operetta presentations (July and August)

AUGUST:
see July

SEPTEMBER:
- Vienna Fair

OCTOBER:
see general events

NOVEMBER:
- Schubert Days
- Antique Fair
- Antique Show in the Kursalon
- Champagne Ball

DECEMBER:
- Advent in Vienna
- Christ Child Market

A detailed calendar of monthly events appears two weeks in advance and is available in all information offices of the Vienna Tourist Service (Wiener Fremdenverkehrsverband).

VIENNESE GUESTS

Visit of Princess Gracia Patricia of Monaco, 1980

ZUR
ERINNERUNG
an den besuch
seiner exzellenz
des bundeskanzlers
der bundesrepublik deutschland
DR · HELMUT KOHL
im rathaus
der bundeshauptstadt
wien
am 21 · november 1984

above left side: Golden Book of the City of Vienna

below left side: President Dr. Richard von Weizsäcker
                         (FRG), 1986

right side above left: King Carl Gustav of Sweden and
                         Queen Silvia, 1979

right side above: Pope John Paul II., 1983

right side below left: Walt Disney, 1962

right side below right: Minister President Nikita Kruschev, 1960

Princess Diana and Prince Charles, 1986

HEURIGER

Almost as celebrated as the coffee house in Vienna is the Heuriger (an establishment where „new wine" is served), a meeting place for young and old where wine and the „Wienerlied" (Viennese song) create an atmosphere of relaxation. Grinzing, Nußdorf, Neustift am Walde, Sievering and Oberlaa are the best-known „Heuriger" regions of Vienna, although Vienna's immediate surroundings boast a great number of Heuriger localities with tradition.

At the typical „Heuriger", only wine or otherwise alcohol-free drinks are served, for example a „Viertel" (1/4 liter) or an „Achtel" (1/8 liter) glass of wine, or a „Gspritzten" (a mixture of red or white wine with mineral- or soda water) – the favorite Viennese drink. A cold buffet consisting of various sandwich spreads, cheese, eggs, and rolls is usually served. The „Wiener Schrammeln" (a special Viennese music style) are an essential part of the „Heuriger" atmosphere in Grinzing, seren-

ading with two violins, a guitar and two accordions, and continuing in the tradition of the Schrammel brothers, successful composers of Viennese music. The „Heurigen" establishments are simply furnished with wooden benches or chairs, and the dishes and cutlery are traditionally rustic. The trademark of the genuine „Heuriger" are a fir-wreath over the entrance and a „Buschenschank" country table. Only those establishments that harvest their own wine in Vienna or in surrounding districts may hold the title of „Heuriger"; the purchase of wine grapes from elsewhere is strictly prohibited. „Heuriger" wine is that which is harvested in September and October of the previous year. After November 11, on Martini's Festival, the „Heuriger" („this year's wine") becomes the „old" wine. Vienna's vineyards cover an area of 720 hectares, farmed by 700 families, and the annual wine harvest amounts to roughly 30,000 hectoliters – or approximately 12 million „Viertel" (1/4 liter glasses).

President of the French Republic François Mitterand, 1982

President Richard ("Tricky Dick") Nixon of the USA, 1956

CULINARY VIENNA

Beside its numerous sights and cultural events, Vienna is worth visiting for its typical cuisine, coffee houses and „Heurigen". A culinary tour of Vienna is a must for even the most demanding connoisseur. „Beisln" (Viennese inns with variegated clientele) and gourmet restaurants offer something for every taste. Despite a rise in popularity of French „light cuisine" in past years, the typical Austrian cuisine has continued to hold its own.

A CULINARY GUIDE THROUGH VIENNA
RESTAURANTS: (LUXUS-CLASS)

Belvedere Stöckl,
3., Prinz-Eugen-Str. 25

Bristol-Korso bei der Oper,
1., Kärntner Ring 1

Hilton-Rotisserie Prinz Eugen,
3., Am Stadtpark

Imperial-Restaurant Württemberg,
1., Kärntner Ring 16

Kervansaray,
1., Mahlerstraße 9

Palais Schwarzenberg,
3., Schwarzenberg Platz 9

Sacher,
1., Philharmonikerstraße 4

Die Savoyengemächer,
15., Schweglerstraße 37

Stadtkrug,
1., Weihburggasse 3

Zu den 3 Husaren,
1., Weihburggasse 10

Parkhotel Schönbrunn,
13., Hietzinger Hauptstr. 10–20

RESTAURANTS:

Eckel,
19., Sieveringer Straße 46

Hauswirth,
16., Otto-Bauer-Gasse 20

Kupferdachl,
1., Schottengasse 7

Niky's Kuchlmasterei,
3., Obere Weißgerberstraße 6

D'Rauchkuchl,
15., Schweglerstr. 37

Bürgerhof,
18., Gentzgasse 127

Donauturm,
22., Donauturmstraße 4

Gösser Bierklinik,
1., Steindlgasse 4

Schiffsrestaurant MFS Theodor Körner,
2., DSG-Schiffsstation, Handelskai 265
(November - February)

COFFEE HOUSES

The Viennese coffee house is a concept associated wordlwide with the city of Vienna. Its genesis is related in two versions: the „historical" version maintains the Emperor Leopold I granted the privilege of serving the Turkish drink to the Armenian Johannes Diodato for a period of twenty years on January 17, 1685. However, the Viennese legend tells of the Turkish siege of 1683, whereby 500 sacks of the brown beans were left behind by the retreating Turkish warriors. Joseph Georg Ko-schitzky of Poland was given these coffee beans by the city of Vienna as a reward for his services during the siege, and he opened his coffee shop „zur blauen Flasche" („The Blue Bottle") in the Donaustraße. At first, the Viennese didn't take very well to the brown beverage, but when Ko-schitsky filtered his coffee and added honey and milk, it started to become popular, and the typically Viennese „melange" was born. The „Kipferl" pastry, in the shape of the Turkish half-moon, supposedly originated at this time. The Viennese coffee house became an established part of the public and social life, the „Mecca of mocca", the „living room of literature". Literary figure Hans Weigl said of the

above left:
Jacky Kennedy, 1961

above right:
Dalai Lama of Tibet, 1986

middle:
Federal Chancellor Dr. Konrad
Adenauer (BRD), 1957

below left:
King Baudouin and
Queen Fabiola of Belgium, 1971

below right:
King Hussein of Jordan, 1980

coffee house: „There, you're neither at home nor out of doors." Otto Friedlaender added: „You can be alone without feeling alone – and this is the Viennese favorite way to be sociable." Coffee House furnishings were originally simple, but the Biedermeier period changed all that. Within a showy and costly atmosphere, card-playing, billiards and chess developed into standard rituals of sociable pastime. The first Viennese coffee house to offer most contemporary magazines and newspapers for reading was the „Kramer'sche Kaffeehaus" in the Schlossergasse next to St. Stephan's cathedral. Neuner's „Silver Coffee House" was also popular, furnished in bright silver. Literary figures such as Franz Grillparzer, Anastasius Grün and Ferdinand Raimund frequented the „Silver Coffee House", as well as prominent businessmen and intellectuals. And in the suburbs, the so-called „Volkskaffee" (public coffee house) or „Tschecherl" was evolving. After 1848, the coffee house became the rendez-vous for those seeking information from newspapers and personal conversation. In the second half of the 19th century, the „literacy coffee house" was especially common, an example of which was the „Griensteidl" near the Hofburg, where contemporary writers such as Arthur Schnitzler, Hofmannsthal or Bahr could be found. Later, the „Cafe Central" hosted Peter Altenberg and friends. The Vienna coffee house had its heyday before World War One. Accord to locality and clientele, different kinds of coffee houses became distinct: for example, there was the „family" coffee house, the „garden" coffee house, coffee houses for billiards, artists, concert-goers, literacy people, the theater and private societies. Today there are approximately 2000 coffee houses in Vienna. The waiter in the coffee house, „Herr Ober", is the essence of the service personnel, and is purportedly capable of knowing each guest's wish at a glance. The most famous modern coffee houses are the „Hawelka" (mentioned in the song by Georg Danzer), „Cafe Landmann", „Central", „Sperl", „Museum",

„Hummel", „Prückel", „Demel", „Raimund" and „Dommayer". Among new-style coffee houses are the „Sirk", the „Cafe am Park" in the Hotel Hilton or the „Coural". However, coffee is not all the same, as the Viennese distinguish between several sorts: Melange, Großer Brauner, Kleiner Brauner, Großer Mokka, Kleiner Mokka, Kaisermelange (black with egg yolk), Kapuziner (small cup of black coffee with cream), Turkish coffee, Mokka gespritzt (black with cognac, brandy or rum), to name a few. A glass of water is served with coffee in all good coffee houses.

COFFEE HOUSES

Cafe *Hawelka*,
1., Dorotheergasse 6

Landtmann,
1., Dr.Karl-Lueger-Ring 4

Central,
1., Herrengasse 14

Sperl,
6., Gumpendorfer Straße 11

Museum,
1., Friedrichstraße 6

Demel,
1., Kohlmarkt 14

Eiles,
8., Josefstädter Straße 2

Hummel,
8., Josefstädter Straße 66

Prückel,
1., Stubenring 24

Raimund,
1., Museumstraße 6

Bräunerhof,
1., Stallburggasse2

Dommayer,
13., Auhofstraße 2

Stadlmann,
9., Währinger Straße 26

Sirk,
1., Kärntner Straße 53

Coural,
8., Josefstädter Straße 35

Alt-Wien,
1., Lugeck 1–2

Frauenhuber,
1.,Himmelpfortgasse 6

Grünwald,
1., Bauernmarkt 10

NIGHT CLUBS

Butterfly,
1., Marc-Aurel-Straße 8

Casanova Revue-Bar,
1., Dorotheergasse 6–8

Chez Nous,
1., Kärntner Durchgang

Club Emanuela
1., Opernring 11

Eve-Bar,
1., Führichgasse 3

Josefine,
1., Sonnenfelsgasse 9

Memory,
1., Schellinggasse 3

Moulin-Rouge,
1., Walfischgasse 11

Renz,
2., Zirkusgasse 50

Evergreen Dancing,
9., Liechtenfelsgasse 31

Marrakesch,
14., Linzer Straße 199

Lolo Bar,
15., Sechshauser Straße 58

Salambo,
17., Hernalser Hauptstraße 20

Cicciolina

The above mentioned restaurants, coffee houses and pubs from a partial list of what Vienna has to offer – although our list is not completely comprehensive, it is recent at the date of printing. There are in Vienna, of course, many restaurants offering a wide variety in international cuisine, such as Chinese, Korean, Indian, French, Italian, Greek, Russian, and vegetarian eateries.

The „Bermuda triangle" in Vienna's inner city, located between Stephansplatz, Rabensteig and Judenplatz, is an area filled with crowded fashionable pubs and small bars – the ideal spot for night owls. Many of these small clubs draw a clientele through the word-of-mouth of satisfied customers. A current address list can be found in the Viennese magazines „Wiener" and „Falter".

above left: Oskar Kokoschka, 1947
above middle: Indian Minister President Indira Gandhi, 1971
above right: Prince Philip of Great Britain, 1981
middle left: Thomas Mann, 1952

middle right: Dr. Silvius Magnago, 1988
below left: King Juan Carlos and Queen Sophie of Spain, 1978
below middle: Vittorio de Sica, Italy, 1958
below right: Minister President Felipe Gonzales Marquez
                (Spain), 1983

Josefine Baker, 1958

Danny Kaye, 1955

SHOPPING IN VIENNA

n the course of the years Vienna has become a first-class shopping city. Designers from all over the world present their fashions here. Vienna's first minicipal district (inner city) presents the most elegant shopping opportunities, in the Kohlmarkt, the Graben and the Kärntnerstraße. The Mariahilferstraße (not far from the Kärntnerstraße) is the longest boulevard of shops in the city. But almost every district in Vienna has a wide variety of stores, for example the pedestrian zone Reumannplatz in the 10th district, the Landstraßer Hauptstraße (3rd district), Simmeringer Hauptstraße (11th district), Meidlinger Hauptstraße (12th district), etc. Among Vienna's well-known marketplaces, the „Naschmarkt" on the Wienzeile is of top rank. Spaced on an area of 36,334 square meters, 150 dealers offer their wares, be it fruits, vegetables, spices, simply everything a gourmet could desire. Vienna boasts numerous antique shops, especially in the narrow lanes of the inner city, where objects of

every kind can be purchased. And in the Dorotheum, the artwork-seeker has a good chance of finding something interesting, either in auctions or through direct purchase. The flea-markets of Vienna offer a cheaper and less staid way of buying old things. The largest flea-market is held Saturdays near the Nachmarkt. Otherwise, most businesses are open Monday–Friday from 9 AM to 6 PM and on Saturdays from 9 AM to 12 PM. Grocery stores open usually before 8 AM, but they close for a noon break between 12.30 PM and 3 PM. Once a month there is a „long shopping Saturday", on the first Saturday of the month, and then the most shops close in the evening. The shops at the west and south train stations (West- und Südbahnhof) are open daily from 7 AM to 11 PM. Tobacconist shops open sometimes as early as 6 AM or earlier.